First published in Great Britain in 2019 by Yellow Kite
An imprint of Hodder & Stoughton
An Hachette UK company

4

Copyright © Eckhart Tolle 2019
Excerpts from *The Power of Now* copyright © Eckhart Tolle 1999

Design by Tracy Cunningham
Cover and interior images used under licence from Shutterstock.com

A CIP catalogue record for this title is available from the British Library

Hardback ISBN 978 1 529 38394 2

Typeset in Scala Regular

Printed and bound in China by C&C Offset Printing Co. , Ltd.

Hodder & Stoughton policy is to use papers that are natural, renewable and recyclable products and made from wood grown in sustainable forests. The logging and manufacturing processes are expected to conform to the environmental regulations of the country of origin.

Yellow Kite
Hodder & Stoughton Ltd
Carmelite House
50 Victoria Embankment
London EC4Y 0DZ

www.yellowkitebooks.co.uk

THE POWER OF
NOW
journal

Eckhart Tolle

When you are on a journey, it is certainly helpful to know where you are going…but don't forget: the only thing that is ultimately real about your journey is *the step that you are taking at this moment.*

Your inner journey only has one step:

the step you are taking right now.

Stay present, stay conscious.
Be the ever-alert guardian
of your inner space.

The good news is that you *can* free yourself from your mind. This is the only true liberation.

You can take the first step right now.

Only the present can free you of the past.
More time cannot free you of time.

Access the power of Now. That is the key.

Is fear preventing you from taking action?

Acknowledge the fear, watch it,

take your attention into it, be fully present with it.

Doing so cuts the link between the fear and your thinking.

I speak of a profound transformation of human consciousness — not as a distant future possibility, but available now — no matter who or where you are.

You shift back and forth for a while between consciousness and unconsciousness, between the state of presence and the state of mind identification.

You lose the Now, and you return to it, again and again. Eventually, presence becomes your predominant state.

Observe the rhythm of your breathing; feel the air flowing in and out, feel the life energy inside your body. Allow everything to be, within and without.

Allow the "isness" of all things. *Move deeply into the Now.*

Be aware of the space that allows everything to be.
Listen to the sounds; don't judge them.

Listen to the silence underneath the sounds. Touch something — anything — and feel and acknowledge its Being.

The moment you start *watching the thinker*, a higher level of consciousness becomes activated. You then begin to realize that there is a vast realm of intelligence beyond thought....

You also realize that all the things that truly matter — beauty, love, creativity, joy, inner peace — arise from beyond the mind.

You begin to awaken.

Attention is the key to transformation — and full attention also implies acceptance. Attention is like a beam of light — the focused power of your consciousness that *transmutes everything into itself.*

To offer no resistance to life is to be in a state of grace, ease, and lightness. This state is then no longer dependent upon things being in a certain way, good or bad.

I cannot tell you any spiritual truth
that deep within you don't know already.
All I can do is *remind you of what you have forgotten.*

You are shown how to free yourself from enslavement
to the mind, enter into this enlightened
state of consciousness and sustain it in everyday life.

The word "enlightenment" conjures up the idea of some super-human accomplishment, and the ego likes to keep it that way, but it is simply your natural state of *felt* oneness with Being.

The present moment holds the key to liberation. But you cannot find the present moment as long as you *are* your mind.

Through forgiveness, which essentially means recognizing the insubstantiality of the past and allowing the present moment to be as it is, the miracle of transformation happens not only within but also without.

If you suddenly feel very light, clear, and deeply at peace, that is an unmistakable *sign that you have truly surrendered.*

Every time you create a gap in the stream of mind,
the light of *your consciousness grows stronger.*

Are you polluting the world or cleaning up the mess?

You are responsible for your inner space; nobody else is, just as you are responsible for the planet.

As within, so without: If humans clear inner pollution,
then they will also cease to create outer pollution.

Non-surrender hardens your psychological form, the shell of the ego, and so creates a strong sense of separateness.

Enlightenment means rising above thought,
not falling back to a level below thought.

Instead of "watching the thinker," you can also create a gap in the mind stream simply by directing the focus of your attention into the Now. Just become *intensely conscious of the present moment.*

Any emotion that you take your presence into
will quickly *subside and become transmuted.*

If you find it hard to enter the Now directly, start by observing the habitual tendency of your mind to want to escape from the Now.

The truth is that the only power there is,
is contained within this moment:
It is the power of your presence.

Ask yourself what "problem" you have right now,
not next year, tomorrow, or five minutes from now.
What is wrong with *this moment*?

Whenever you notice that some form of negativity has
arisen within you, look on it not as a failure,
but as a helpful signal that is telling you:
"Wake up. Get out of your mind. Be present."

Observe the many ways in which unease, discontent, and tension arise within you through unnecessary judgment, resistance to what *is*, and denial of the Now.

I was awakened by the chirping of a bird outside the window.
I had never heard such a sound before.

My eyes were still closed, and I saw the image of a precious diamond. *Yes, if a diamond could make a sound, this is what it would be like.*

If you have lived long enough, you will know that things
"go wrong" quite often. It is precisely at those times
that surrender needs to be practiced if you want to
eliminate pain and sorrow from your life.

Always say "yes" to the present moment. Surrender to what *is*. Say "yes" to life — and see how life suddenly starts working for you rather than against you.

It has been said that nothing in this world is so like God as silence. All you have to do is *pay attention to it.*

What is stillness other than presence,
consciousness freed from thought forms?

There are many ways to create a gap in the incessant stream of thought. This is what meditation is all about.

Even if there is noise, there is always some silence underneath and in between the sounds. Listening to the silence *immediately creates stillness inside you.*

Presence is pure consciousness — consciousness that has been reclaimed from the mind, from the world of form.

No other life-form on the planet knows negativity, only humans, just as no other life-form violates and poisons the Earth that sustains it.

It is essential to bring more consciousness into your life
in ordinary situations when everything
is going relatively smoothly. In this way,
you grow in presence power.

Compassion is the awareness of a deep bond
between yourself and all creatures.

Become an alchemist. Transmute base metal into gold, suffering into consciousness, disaster into enlightenment.

Watch any plant or animal and let it teach you
acceptance of what is, surrender to the Now.
Let it teach you Being.

Glimpses of love and joy or brief moments of deep peace are possible whenever a gap occurs in the stream of thought.

The first light of dawn was filtering through the curtains.
Without any thought, I felt, I knew,
that there is infinitely more to light than we realize.

That soft luminosity filtering through the
curtains was love itself.

Use your senses fully: Be where you are. Look around — just look, don't interpret. See the light, shapes, colors, textures. *Be aware of the silent presence of each thing.*

Make it a habit to ask yourself:
What's going on inside me at this moment?
That question will point you in the right direction.

Problems are mind-made and need time to survive.
They cannot survive in the actuality of the Now.
Focus your attention on the Now and tell me
what problem you have at this moment.

Forget about your life situation and pay attention to your *life*. Your life situation exists in time. Your life is now. Your life situation is mind-stuff. *Your life is real.*

It is a silent but intense presence that dissolves
the unconscious patterns of the mind.
They may still remain active for a while,
but they won't run your life anymore.

There is nothing that you need to understand
before you can become present.

When you wash your hands, pay attention
to all the sense perceptions associated with the activity:
the sound and feel of the water, the movement of your hands,
the scent of the soap, and so on.

Nothing ever happened in the past; it happened in the Now.
Nothing will ever happen in the future;
it will happen in the Now.

Enlightenment consciously chosen means to relinquish
your attachment to past and future and to
make the Now the main focus of your life.

When you become conscious of Being, what is really
happening is that Being becomes conscious of itself.
When Being becomes conscious of itself — *that's presence.*

Joy is uncaused and arises from within as the joy of Being.
It is an essential part of the inner state of peace,
the state that has been called the peace of God.

It is your natural state, not something that you need
to work hard for or struggle to attain.

Body awareness keeps you present. It anchors you in the Now.

Since all worlds are interconnected,

when collective human consciousness becomes transformed,

nature and the animal kingdom will reflect that transformation. *This points to the possibility of a completely different order of reality.*

To know yourself as the Being underneath the thinker,
the stillness underneath the mental noise,
the love and joy underneath the pain,
is freedom, salvation, enlightenment.

Presence removes time.

Without time, no suffering, no negativity, can survive.

With practice, the sense of stillness and peace will deepen.
In fact, there is no end to its depth.
You will also feel a subtle emanation of
joy arising from deep within: the joy of Being.

That stillness and vastness that enables
the universe to *be*…is also within you.
When you are utterly and totally present, you encounter
it as the still inner space of no-mind.

There is nothing you can ever do or attain
that will get you closer to salvation than it is at this moment.
This may be hard to grasp for a mind accustomed to
thinking that everything worthwhile is in the future.

When you live in complete acceptance of what *is*, that is the *end of all drama in your life.*

If you withdraw attention from *things* — objects in
space — you automatically withdraw attention from your
mind objects as well. In other words: You cannot think
and *be aware of space — or of silence.*

Love is a state of Being. Your love is not outside; it is deep within you. You can never lose it, and it cannot leave you. It is not dependent on some other body, some external form.

Your peace is so vast and deep that anything that is not peace disappears into it as if it had never existed.

Everybody you come in contact with will be touched by your presence and affected by the peace that you emanate, *whether they are conscious of it or not.*

About the Author

World-renowned spiritual teacher Eckhart Tolle conveys simple wisdom that transcends any particular religion, doctrine, or guru. His #1 *New York Times* bestselling book *The Power of Now* is a modern classic in the field of personal growth and spirituality. His other books include *A New Earth* and *Stillness Speaks*. He lives in Vancouver, British Columbia. For upcoming events, books, and audios and videos of Eckhart's seminars, visit his website.

EckhartTolle.com

yellow kite

books to help you live a good life

Join the conversation and tell
us how you live a #goodlife

🐦 @yellowkitebooks

📘 YellowKiteBooks

📌 Yellow Kite Books

📷 YellowKiteBooks